God in My Business

Julia A. Royston

BK Royston Publishing
P. O. Box 4321
Jeffersonville, IN 47131
502-802-5385
http://www.bkroystonpublishing.com
bkroystonpublishing@gmail.com

© Copyright – 2020

All Rights Reserved. No part of this book may be reproduced, stored in a retrieval system, or transmitted by any means without the written permission of the author.

Cover Design: Gad Savage, Elite Covers
Cover Photo: Lori A. Hobbs

ISBN-13: 978-1-951941-42-0

King James Version Scriptural Text – Public Domain
New International Version (NIV) - Holy Bible, New International Version®, NIV® Copyright ©1973, 1978, 1984, 2011 by Biblica, Inc.® Used by permission. All rights reserved worldwide.

Printed in the United States of America

Dedication

I dedicate this book to entrepreneurs who love God and want God in their business.

God is concerned about your business too.

Let's go!

Acknowledgements

First, I acknowledge my Lord and Savior Jesus Christ for giving me all of my gifts and especially my gift to write His words.

My husband who is always supportive, loving and encouraging me to utilize all of my gifts and talents. Thank you honey.

To my mother, Dr. Daisy Foree, who is my number one cheerleader and always tells me, "hang in there, you can do it." To my father, Dr. Jack Foree, who is never far away from me in spirit or my heart. I only have to look in the mirror each day to see him.

To Rev. Claude and Mrs. Lillie Royston who support me in everything I do. Especially, Rev. Royston for his careful eye to detail and his sensitive heart to content.

To the rest of my family, I love you and thank you for your prayers, support and love.

Table of Contents

Dedication	iii
Acknowledgements	v
Introduction	xi
Where is Your Towel?	1
Who Do You Serve?	5
Always Do This!	9
First Things First	13
Time Alone	17
Perspective and Reputation	21
What Do You Do?	25
A Man's Gift	29
He's Not Taking It Back	33
Right Relationship with Money	37
Power to Get Wealth is From God	41
Rise Up Early	45
What's the Plan?	49

Where's the Path?	53
Follow Me	59
Moved with Compassion	63
Act Immediately	67
Where are the People?	71
Priorities – The Law of Firsts	75
The Succession Plan	79
Mentoring and Being Mentored	83
Who Is on Your Team?	87
Platform, Performance, and Purpose	93
How Do You See Yourself?	99
Count up the Cost	103
It Costs – There is an Investment	107
Faith in a Storm	111
The Dry Season	115
What Do You See?	119
Launch	123

Other Resources By This Author   127

About the Author   128

Introduction

We have all heard the saying that there should be a separation of "church and state" but for me and my business, God and Business go hand and hand. I have always inserted spirituality, hope and faith into my books but this is my first book that is clearly intentional about God being in my Business.

I was challenged by my business bestie, Vanessa Collins to write this book. She knows how much I enjoy writing and honestly, it came quite easy to me. God gave me the 30 scriptures directly from my experience. Thankfully, Biblegateway.com for clarifying and giving me the correct scriptural text and passage.

My challenge to each of you that read this book to pray to God about your business. He is the creator, best idea giver and master of all things. Ask Him. Seek Him and Find out His Plan and Advice for you, your life and your business every day.

Know that you'll be the divine success you were designed to be when you have God in Your Business.

Let's go to work!
Julia Royston

Where is Your Towel?

"He riseth from supper, and laid aside his garments; and took a towel, and girded himself. After that he poureth water into a bason, and began to wash the disciples' feet, and to wipe them with the towel wherewith he was girded." John 13:4-5 (KJV)

One of the most humbling things that Jesus ever did was wash the disciples' feet. In those days, they walked everywhere. Horses, chariots, people, animals, discarded food, and everything else you can imagine in those days, was by the side of the road. People's feet were dirty. The first thing that was done in a person's home for a visitor was to greet them and wash their feet. It's a dirty job. It probably wasn't done by the owner of the house, but someone else did it.

As a publisher, I have realized that books are my client's babies, dreams, hopes, and ultimate goal in life. I must feel what they are feeling. I must be able to get down into the story with them. Some stories are messy, dirty, painful, and uncomfortable but my business is also ministry. So, it sometimes requires me to come out of my comfort zone, lay aside my garment, wash their feet of the stinky mindset, hurt, pain, grief, and sorrow that many of my client's face before we ever get to the book idea, or sign a contract, or do business. If, as entrepreneur, the job is dirty and sometimes not fun, be willing to do what is legal, moral and ethical to bless and help your clients so that you can, ultimately, receive the reward of showing Christ that you can be trusted with the business you are in. So, before you get the bag, open up the bank account, or draw up the business plan, where is your towel?

Affirmation: God help me to always be willing to humble myself and minister to the people that I will encounter. In Jesus' name. Amen.

Question: What does your towel, or a description of serving others look like for you and your business?

_____
_____
_____
_____
_____
_____
_____
_____
_____
_____
_____
_____
_____
_____
_____
_____
_____
_____

Reflection and Planning

_____
_____
_____
_____
_____
_____
_____
_____
_____
_____
_____
_____
_____
_____
_____

Who Do You Serve?

"But he that is greatest among you shall be your servant." Matthew 23:11 (KJV)

Who serves you and who are you serving? Jesus said that the greatest among us is the servant. Who do you serve? When someone calls me for services the first thing I ask is, "How can I help you?" Yes, I have a for profit business, but my job is to serve them and help them get their project completed and released to the world. If my service is correct, on point, and to their satisfaction, I'll have more clients. I'll have more customers because they will return and bring friends, and acquaintances with them. But if you don't know how to serve to the benefit of your customer, client, or even your employees or independent contractor, you won't be successful.

On the other hand, coaches, and especially business coaches, will tell you to write down the avatar or the description of your ideal client, and the person you most likely want to work with and serve. For a Christian entrepreneur, that can be tricky because God may, as a test, send someone your way, who doesn't fit that ideal client that you said that you wanted to work with. My next question is not so easy. Service grows with time, effort, and availability, and will move from who do you serve now or who do you want to serve in the future; but my next question really is, Who will you serve?

I was at an event once and a gentleman came up to me and was showing me his manuscript and samples of what he wanted to write. Someone at my table said, "He probably doesn't have any money to pay you for your services. He looks like a homeless man." I told them, "Looks can be deceiving. That man has a doctorate, oversees hundreds of clients, and runs a multi-million dollar organization." Further, he did do business with me and paid in full, no payment plan.

As Christians, God is our master and we worship HIM only, but in business and at times, we will be the hands, feet, service, and ministry that He will use to bless others and to be blessed ourselves. The greatest is the servant. Who do you serve?

Affirmation: God help me to keep my eyes and heart open to serve those that you place in my sphere of influence. Give me discernment to know the heart and the spirit rather than the outward appearance. In Jesus' name. Amen.

Question: Who do you currently serve or one day desire to serve?

_____
_____
_____
_____
_____
_____
_____
_____
_____
_____
_____
_____
_____
_____
_____
_____

Always Do This!

> "And he spake a parable unto them to this end, that men ought always to pray, and not to faint;"
> Luke 18:1 (KJV)

Rule #1 is ask God. Entrepreneurship is hard work and not for the faint of heart. I will probably repeat that throughout this book in more ways than one, because it is not for the faint of heart. Even if you feel like you are a pretty strong person there will come things your way on this journey that will test that, but "pray without ceasing." Pray about everything. Pray about everyone. Pray about every move. Pray about the next 'big' idea, and seek God. People who are gifted sometimes rely on their gift for their next move. Some moves are obvious, but in this season, there are things after the next move, around the bend, over the river, and through the woods, that you don't know yet, but God knows.

Find your space. Find your time. Be consistent in your prayer time with God. It will make all of the difference in the world.

Affirmation: God I thank you that I can pray to you about everything. In Jesus' name. Amen.

Question: How much time do you spend praying each day?

Reflection and Planning

_____
_____
_____
_____
_____
_____
_____
_____
_____
_____
_____
_____
_____
_____
_____
_____
_____

First Things First

"Seek Ye First the Kingdom and All these other things will be added unto you. But seek ye first the kingdom of God, and his righteousness; and all these things shall be added unto you." Matthew 6:33 (KJV)

There are times that you will have to remind yourself of this every day, every hour, and every minute of the day and that is to *Seek* first the Kingdom. The Kingdom of God is "Not meat and drink" which are the things that satisfy the flesh and outward man, but "righteousness, peace, joy in the Holy Ghost." Romans 14:17 (KJV) The inner man, through the Holy Ghost or the Holy Spirit, whichever you are most familiar, must be, and continually must be built and stabilized on a firm foundation. Otherwise, your business, your life, and family will crumble. Make sure that you slow down, put it in your schedule, or start out your day with those things that will increase and build up the Kingdom of God inside of you before you can fight against the kingdoms of this world, the enemy, poverty, and controversial clients. There will be temptations to compromise, deceive, and not to walk in integrity, but when you have the reassurance that all of heaven and the King of Kings is on your side, and will take care of you and your business, it will make all the difference in the world.

Seek first the Kingdom and everything else will be added unto you. First things First!

Affirmation: God I seek your righteousness, peace and joy for my soul and life, knowing that you will take care of everything else. In Jesus' name. Amen.

Question: Where is your best or favorite place to seek first things first?

_____
_____
_____
_____
_____
_____
_____
_____
_____
_____
_____
_____
_____
_____
_____
_____
_____
_____
_____
_____

Reflection and Planning

_____
_____
_____
_____
_____
_____
_____
_____
_____
_____
_____
_____
_____
_____
_____

Time Alone

"And when he had sent the multitudes away, he went up into a mountain apart to pray: and when the evening was come, he was there alone." Matthew 14:23 (KJV)

It is amazing that in this scripture Jesus went to pray, but in the second half of the scripture verse it specifically says that he was there alone. Now you may say, "I'm never alone because He is with me." That is true, but there are some times and hopefully on a daily basis that you take time to be alone. Alone with God! Alone with your thoughts! Alone to just sit and clear your mind of the outside noise of your business world! There are times that you do need to be alone. Alone to collect yourself from the tasks, assignments and duties of your business and the world! Sometimes you have to be alone and do, think, or say nothing at all. Alone! The biggest extrovert needs some time alone. The introverts of this world must have it, and crave it to survive, but we all need that time alone. Today we call it 'me time.' At times, I get in the car and run errands alone, no music, no radio, and no sound in the car but silence. I know that maybe hard for some, but it is good for you. It helps clear the air. Your ear gate is bombarded with so much information, data, and to do lists that at times you don't know what to do first. That old hymn comes to mind, "I come to the garden alone." Nobody else! Just alone! Find that time, and over time as your business grows, you'll have to schedule that time because you are going to need time alone, just you by yourself.

Affirmation: God, I thank you for the ability to be alone with you. I don't have to talk because you know everything and understand my silence. Thank you for being you. In Jesus' name. Amen.

Question: How much time during the week do you actually spend alone?

Reflection and Planning

Perspective and Reputation

"…He asked them, saying, Whom say the people that I am?" Luke 9:18 (KJV)

I asked my husband once, "What do people get when they do business with me?" He gave his perspective on my reputation, especially since my business had begun to grow. I am a service business, so service is key and providing that service that satisfies people is key to staying in business and for the business to grow. So, it was a valid question, "What do people get when they do business with me?" Now in the scripture, Jesus asked it a different way, "Whom say the people that I am?" In other words, what is my reputation or what is the perception of me in the crowd and the community? I'm sorry, but if Jesus wanted to know, you should want to know. Why are people drawn to you? Why do people do business with you? What is your reputation and their perspective of you as a business owner? It has been said that people do business with people that they 'know, like, and trust.' Are you likeable? Are you trustworthy? Do people know you and don't want to do business with you? Your public perception must be considered and known. If you say, "I don't care what people think about me or what they say about me." I'm sorry, but that shouldn't be the truth even if it is the truth. You should care. Jesus cared and so should you. It is key to your growth, development, and effectiveness as a business owner. It matters! You may not want to face it nor hear the answers. You may not even want to make the changes necessary to address the criticism, but it will make the difference in "being in business" or "going out of business."

Affirmation: Thank you, God, that you asked the question so that I can ask the question, and be the kind of business owner building the business that you designed for me. Help me to change, revise, and refocus myself and my business perception and reputation. In Jesus' name. Amen.

Question: What is your business reputation, or what do you want your business reputation to be?

Reflection and Planning

What Do You Do?

"And he shall be like a tree planted by the rivers of water, that bringeth forth his fruit in his season; his leaf also shall not wither; and whatsoever he doeth shall prosper." Psalm 1:3 (KJV)

I cannot tell you how many times I have been at networking events, introductions to webinar, and tele summits, as well as vending at live events, and they have asked me, "So what do you guys do?" That's a loaded question for me because I do a lot, but an all-important question in business is, Why? That is because people are determining if they have a need for the service or for doing what you actually do. Is that service that you perform, or the thing that you actually do, a complement, accompaniment, or strength necessary to their existing weakness in their business? In my case, people who read buy books. People who want to write a book take my card, and even people who know people who want to write a book take my card and pass it on.

So, my advice to you is, know exactly what you do in your business. Get it down to a one sentence response so that people will know in a concise way what it is, so they can make a decision to go further with the conversation or even schedule a meeting, or discovery call. This concise sentence is what is sometimes called your "elevator pitch" something that can be said in 30 seconds or less. Mine is "Hello, I am Julia Royston of BK Royston Publishing and we help you write, publish, promote, and produce products that will get your message to the masses, turn your words into wealth, and build businesses and platforms."

Affirmation: Thank you God that you and I know that you will prosper whatever I do for your Kingdom and your people. In Jesus' name. Amen.

Question: What do you do?

Reflection and Planning

A Man's Gift

"A man's gift maketh room for him, and bringeth him before great men." Proverbs 18:16 (KJV)

We all love presents and gifts given on any occasion, or no occasion at all. We just love it! I know that I love receiving gifts. It is the thought that counts. I don't really care what it is: whether a cookie, cupcake, or candle, I know that you thought of me. God did the same thing when He gave you the gift that you possess. He thought of you specifically. He carefully selected the gift that He placed inside of you, for free. Whether you recognize it or not, there is a gift inside of you waiting to come out. Additionally, that gift when you display it, will make room, giving space for you to share it, and I believe it will profit you when done in excellence. I also believe that the truly gifted people will never be broke a day in their lives. Your gift is designed to prosper and be a source of profit for you. So, ask yourself, "What is my gift?" Most people who can't answer that question right there, remain stalled, or are stagnant in many areas of their life. At times, other people have to acknowledge, or tell them what their gift is for them to recognize it and own it.

In business, you need to know, and understand how you are gifted, because this is the key to what type of business you will begin, how the business will operate, the people and their characteristics that you will hire on your team, and how and when your business will grow.

Affirmation: I thank you Father that you have placed a gift down inside of me. Help me to display this gift in a way that pleases you and edifies the people that receive it. In Jesus' name. Amen.

Question: What is your gift?

Reflection and Planning

_____
_____
_____
_____
_____
_____
_____
_____
_____
_____
_____
_____
_____
_____
_____
_____
_____

He's Not Taking It Back

"For the gifts and calling of God are without repentance." Romans 11:29 (KJV)

A gift from God is different than a gift from the store. You can't take it back. You can try to hide it but somehow it will spill out. You can try not to tell someone about it but there will be another gifted person in discernment, who will tell you about your gift that you are trying to hide and not use. Gifts and callings of God come without repentance. He is not taking it back. It is a part of your DNA, soul, and spirit. Sorry, it is yours whether you like it or not. Jeremiah said it was like fire shut up in his bones. Now, I know that you are asking, "What does that have to do with business?" Everything! Once you accept what your gift is and how it works, you will know right away what your gift is not: then you can go find the best people to do, and perform that gift that you don't possess. With regards to the gift that you do have, there are three things that I admonish any gifted person to do:

1. Respect the Gift - Once you acknowledge the gift that you have, there has to be a level of respect for that gift. If someone gave you something that you cherish and love, you wouldn't put it just anywhere, you don't let everybody touch it, and you don't let just anybody access it. If you do that with a physical or natural gift, you should do the same or more with the gift God has given you. That business you have started, or that He is asking you to start, must be respected, guarded, and protected at all costs. It is a gift, don't treat it any kind of way.
2. Retool the Gift - Even though the gift is free, the maintenance and upkeep of that gift is not always free. I am a singer, as well as an entrepreneur. Even though one of my natural gifts is to sing, I took voice lessons, participated in choirs, and had a voice teacher so I could understand, train,

and know how to use my gift in the best way possible. It has served me well.

3. Reproduce - Once you've had a level of success or failure in anything, you know it well enough to teach it. Experience is the best teacher. There will be opportunity that will come to you, and if not, create the opportunity to help someone else. You have a responsibility as a Christian business owner, and human being, to help the next person coming up, going through, or even stuck, in their business or life.

He's not taking back the gift that He gave you, so use it to the fullest for His Glory and for the edification of the Kingdom and Community.

Affirmation: Thank you, Lord, that you have blessed me with this gift. No matter the hardship, help me to respect, and love you enough to retool and reproduce this gift in someone else. In Jesus' name. Amen.

Question: What is the most undesirable thing about the gift that He gave you?

_____
_____
_____
_____
_____
_____
_____
_____
_____
_____
_____
_____
_____
_____
_____
_____

Right Relationship with Money

"Money answereth all things. A feast is made for laughter, and wine maketh merry: but money answereth all things." Ecclesiastes 10:19 (KJV)

God spoke to me more than 15 years ago and it transformed my life, and the way I spent money. You have to come to the conclusion that money is a means to an end. Used correctly, money can help grow, expand, and prosper a business, and your life. Of course, the accompanying scripture that always comes up is that "the love of money is the root of all evil." Yes, we don't worship money or love it above God or anything else, but we need money for living, for ministry, and for business. Money truly answers all things. The answer to the thing that we need, that the money can bring, will also depend on the people who are controlling, and issuing the money. Thus, we need a right relationship with money. In business, this is one of the hardest lessons to learn. I had to determine that I wanted to be in a 'For Profit' business rather than a non-profit business, so I had to learn how to charge people for my services. I had to learn how to spend the money, and where it should be allocated when they paid me. Then over time I learned how to save, when to buy other services, and when to save and do the service myself. It is complicated, and you will make mistakes along the way, but first things first; understand your relationship with money. Are you good with money, and have a good working relationship with money, or are you terrible with money? Do you need someone else to handle the money that you are able to accumulate? Do you need an adviser to help you to know when to spend money, and not save it all and still not grow your business? It is a fine balance, and one that as a business owner you must learn quickly, or you will be out of business.

Affirmation: Father help me to be wise and have a good working relationship with money for the sake of my business and my life. In Jesus' name. Amen.

Question: What is your relationship with money.

_____
_____
_____
_____
_____
_____
_____
_____
_____
_____
_____
_____
_____
_____
_____
_____
_____

Power to Get Wealth is From God

"But thou shalt remember the Lord thy God: for it is He that giveth thee power to get wealth, that He may establish His covenant which He sware unto thy fathers, as it is this day." Deuteronomy 8:18 (KJV)

No matter how successful you are, how much money you collect, or how high your net worth gets, remember it is God who gives us the Power to Get Wealth. The power, strength, and ability to get wealth, for a Christian, comes from God. We cannot do it by ourselves. We did not just think of those bright ideas by ourselves; God did it, and God brought it. God gives us the power, but it is now time for us to put in the work. He is NOT going to do that part for us. You have the gifts, talents, and abilities as well as the connections, and people to do what He called you to do. There will be things that arise that you may, or may not be prepared for, and that require work, and faith; but you don't stop just because it gets hard. You don't stop because you don't know something: go ask, and figure it out. You don't stop because it takes you out of your comfort zone. God will continue to give you power, and your job is to trust Him and put forth the effort.

Affirmation: I thank you Father that you have given me power to get wealth. Lead me, and guide me to the people, places, and provisions that you have for me. In Jesus' name. Amen.

Question: What has God instructed you to do, or given you access to, that you haven't done yet?

_____

_____

_____

_____

_____

_____

_____

_____

_____

_____

_____

_____

_____

_____

_____

Reflection and Planning

_____
_____
_____
_____
_____
_____
_____
_____
_____
_____
_____
_____
_____
_____
_____
_____
_____
_____

Rise Up Early

"..She gets up while it is still night;"
Proverbs 31:15 (NIV)

This devotional is not to point fingers at anyone's sleep habits, but there is something special about getting up early. You may be one who stays up late, and sleeps late: if that works for you, congratulations. But for most successful entrepreneurs that I know, they are up early in the mornings. If they are up really late at night, there is a valid reason, project, or deadline that they have to meet. I know that this scripture is from the Proverbs 31 woman, but David says, in Psalm 63:1, "O God, thou art my God; early will I seek thee..." So, not only do the women rise up early, this man rose up early to seek God, as well. You have to determine your own schedule, and use your own judgement, but here are my three reasons why I rise up early.

1. It is quiet, and I am able to pray and seek God first thing, and early.
2. He gives me instruction, ideas, and intelligence for my day.
3. I am able to organize and get leftover items done before 9 a.m. when most businesses begin their workday. I can make early contact with businesses which provide information and resources necessary for me to accomplish the goals of my own business.

My parents said I was an early riser as a baby, so it is natural for me to get up early, but if there is an event for which I have to stay up late, I don't perform well. I know it, and have to take a nap sometime during the day so I can be my best in a late evening event. Adjustments have to be made for success. Your sleep pattern may have to be one of the adjustments that you make because, the "early bird gets the…." You know the rest.

Affirmation. Father help me to not only seek you early in the day, but early and first in every project. In Jesus' name. Amen.

Question: How early do you rise each day?

_____

_____

_____

_____

_____

_____

_____

_____

_____

_____

_____

_____

_____

_____

_____

_____

What's the Plan?

"For I know the plans I have for you, 'declares the Lord,' plans to prosper you and not to harm you, plans to give you hope and a future." Jeremiah 29:11 (NIV)

I'm a planner by nature. I like to be prepared. I like to be organized, thus my librarian background. I have been on teams to organize events for years: but for the plans God has for each of us, He only gives us the promise that He has a plan. He won't leave us. Walk by faith. He doesn't give us all of the details all at once, because at times we couldn't handle the details. Know that He has a plan, but sometimes, we have to be prepared for the plan. There are some prerequisites, or lessons that we have to learn first before we are ready for the plan that God is about to implement. He has it all worked out. He has it all planned out. He knows who you are going to need to meet, the where, the when, the how, and what role they will play in carrying out His perfect plan. Your job is to keep praying, listening, and obeying.

This devotional is probably for me even more than you, because I have to keep reminding myself that God is the creator, author, finisher, provider, sustainer, and planner of my life. He's got this. My life is in His hands, not mine. Some days I am asked, "What's the plan?" I can clearly answer, "I don't know, but I know that God knows."

Affirmation: Thank you, God, that you have the plan, provision, and people for my life. Help me to seek you first and obey your instructions. In Jesus' name. Amen.

Question: What was the last plan that God gave you?

Reflection and Planning

_____
_____
_____
_____
_____
_____
_____
_____
_____
_____
_____
_____
_____
_____
_____

Where's the Path?

"Teach me thy way, O Lord, and lead me in a plain path, because of mine enemies." Psalm 27:11 (KJV)

I was hired to work at a Fortune 500 company. The best job of my life. After only 9 months, into the job, God said, "Go home." I was like, I am home, and I lived only 5 minutes from my job. It was awesome. I was trying to make a deal with God, but it didn't work. He won! I moved back home after only a year on that job. I was devasted. I had to take a more than $20,000 a year pay cut. I went from a private office, key card access to the building, and a code access to my office, to a private high school library in an all-girls school. My ego, self-esteem, and pride in myself, hit the bottom of the ground. I even tried to go back to the company. However, the entire department I was in, was dismantled amid criminal charges for corporate espionage from a superior. Huh? God knew the correct path that

I should take, but I didn't know. I didn't know that the path that I was on may have ended into having to search for a new job, and/or not finding a job at all in my field because I didn't follow His path. Who leaves a corporate job to be an entrepreneur? You may have, but you heard from God, and He has the plan, and the path. So, follow Him! It won't make sense to others, but God knows everything, and why He wants you on that path.

I didn't have much money in those years when I returned home but I was always provided for, and what I didn't receive in money, I received in much training, and a free Master's Degree. It may not look like much, but make sure that you are following God's path, and it will turn out, not always feeling good, or looking good, or being an easy road, but it will turn out for your good!

Affirmation: Thank you, God; you have the path and direction that I should go in my life. Help me to find it and walk swiftly on it without complaint. In Jesus' name. Amen.

Question 1: God's way is the best way. Have you ever gone your way and seen the way God wanted you to go, and were disappointed?

_____
_____
_____
_____
_____
_____
_____
_____
_____
_____
_____
_____
_____
_____
_____
_____

Question 2: Write about it. What was the mistake that you made?

Reflection and Planning

_____
_____
_____
_____
_____
_____
_____
_____
_____
_____
_____
_____
_____
_____
_____
_____
_____

Follow Me

"And he saith unto them, Follow me, and I will make you fishers of men." Matthew 4:19 (KJV)

I wrote a song once that says, "Follow me, stay with me, abide with me always, You will see victory, If you just Follow Me." This song was written based on the above scripture. The key to the scripture and the song is "Follow Me." If God is truly going to be in our business, we have to follow Him. He will lead us and give us direction if we stay behind Him and follow. The problem, usually, is when He tells us to do something that doesn't agree with the crowd, make sense to the human understanding, or even look like it will be profitable to our living. However, in the end, if we keep walking with God and doing it like He said, it will work out perfectly. Every new fad, event, program, or course is not necessarily for us. We can invest in everything that we want or even need, when we want to do it, if we are following God's leading and direction. We may look like a fool but in the end, remember you are following the King of Kings and the Lord of Lords. Nobody is greater than that. Keep following!

Affirmation: Father God, give me the strength to keep following close behind you. Where you lead me, help me to follow. In Jesus' name. Amen.

Question: When was the last time God told you to do something, go somewhere, or avail yourself to someone; which seemed foolish but worked out perfectly?

Reflection and Planning

_____
_____
_____
_____
_____
_____
_____
_____
_____
_____
_____
_____
_____
_____
_____
_____

Moved with Compassion

"And Jesus went forth, and saw a great multitude, and was moved with compassion" Matthew 14:14 (KJV)

Sometimes I am asked about the publishing industry, or any business for that matter. However, unless you understand fully that the book, product, project, or problem that the person wants, or thinks that you can solve, is of the utmost importance to them and not just a check for you, don't go into business. You must be about your business, but you must have compassion on the people that you are called to, drawn to, and have a connection with; so, it is about service and not just for the incentive to make money. In this scripture, the people were hungry, they had a need and Jesus was moved with compassion to get a way to feed them. People will be hungry for what you have to offer. People will be hungry for the gift that you possess. People will be hungry, and concerned with a serious problem or pain point that they want solved. Your job is to move with compassion, understanding and empathy to solve that problem in a beneficial way to both of you. If you cannot solve the problem or meet the need, tell them the truth, and move forward. Being compassionate is not just a phony way to connive people into paying you money, but that compassion should include integrity, honesty, and hope for a solution.

Affirmation: Father, help me to see a need and move with compassion to help solve the need without moving with greed or dishonesty. In Jesus' name. Amen.

Question: What moves you to compassion for someone else?

Reflection and Planning

Act Immediately

"And immediately Jesus stretched forth his hand…"
Matthew 14:31 (KJV)

One of the critical characteristics of leadership is to be able to act immediately. Disasters would be curtailed, emergencies would be better controlled, and problems would be easier solved and not made worse if we find a solution and act immediately. Act with wisdom, with an understanding of the consequences, and with the weighing of every option, but in the end, you have to act, and hopefully it is immediately. Why? A situation that is critical or of urgency must be acted upon, because it can be the difference between life or death for you and your business. Sure, there are some things that you can wait on: that new car, a new building, or luxury items, but some decisions require your immediate action. There are many cases in the Bible, where Jesus acted and immediately something changed.

What have you been delaying, procrastinating, and waiting around to do? It is getting worse and you are watching it get worse. You're wasting time, money and effort because you will not act. It is a loss, not a gain when you delay. If you don't know what to do, that's one thing. If what you want to do is the wrong thing, that is something else. However, when you know what must be done, and you have the provision, people, plan, and path, put the plan in drive and get it done. Don't wait! If nothing else, act like Jesus, and do it immediately.

Affirmation: I thank you, God, that you act immediately on major areas of my life. I am grateful and appreciate all that you do for me. Help me to act on your command as quickly as you do for me. In Jesus' name. Amen.

Question: What are you waiting on?

Reflection and Planning

Where are the People?

> "Now when Jesus saw great multitudes about him…" Matthew 8:19 (KJV)

Jesus was healing, delivering, and setting people free. He had a great multitude that followed him in the streets. We are now in the virtual, digital, and online streets. We have a great task ahead of us to draw attraction, to engage, and to communicate with a multitude. Wherever Jesus went, He drew a crowd or multitude because He had something that people wanted and needed.

What do you have already, or what can you produce that people need right now? If you don't know, ask them. Jesus didn't have to ask; He could and would look upon their faces and knew exactly what they needed.

You will need customers and clients to stay in business. Determine who you want to serve, and look for the multitude.

Affirmation: Thank you, God, that you are going to send the people to me, and that I am an answer to someone's need. Help me to have compassion, empathy, business with integrity, and love for my fellow man. In Jesus' name. Amen.

Question: Who do you want to serve? What will you offer?

_____
_____
_____
_____
_____
_____
_____
_____
_____
_____
_____
_____
_____
_____
_____
_____
_____
_____
_____
_____

Reflection and Planning

_____
_____
_____
_____
_____
_____
_____
_____
_____
_____
_____
_____
_____
_____
_____
_____
_____
_____

Priorities – The Law of Firsts

"Thou shalt not delay to offer the first of thy ripe fruits, and of thy liquors: the firstborn of thy sons shalt thou give unto me." Exodus 22:29 (KJV)

My first priority each day is to be thankful and grateful to God just to be alive to see another day. My bathroom is my altar, sanctuary, and war room to start my day. It may sound gross to you but God speaks to me there. I am vulnerable there, but I'm also seeking Him there and that is where He meets me. I am grateful.

For an entrepreneur and especially a solopreneur (working alone with little or no staff, not even contractors) you are on a constant roller coaster ride thinking of what to do first. Each day I may start out with a list of what I will do and in what order I will do them. However, a call, email, text message, and/or inbox from social media can change all of that.

I realize that our first priority is to God, His people, plan and provision, combined with prayer, praise, and giving of our first fruits. In this same scripture, I realize that as an oldest child, the firstborn, that I am an offering unto God as well. We all are, but in this scripture specifically, 'the firstborn of thy sons' is an offering up to God, a priority to God, and even under the current dispensation of Grace, the law still applies. In everything that you do, offering up to God your first of the day, month, year, and your life, is of the utmost importance. As you are planning, preparing, and producing, remember that God wants your first.

Affirmation: God, help me to put first things first in my planning, preparation, and provision. Help me to realize that if I put you first, you have me in every area of my life. In Jesus' name. Amen.

Question: What are your top five priorities?

Reflection and Planning

_____
_____
_____
_____
_____
_____
_____
_____
_____
_____
_____
_____
_____
_____
_____

The Succession Plan

"And it came to pass, when they were gone over, that Elijah said unto Elisha, Ask what I shall do for thee, before I be taken away from thee. And Elisha said, I pray thee, let a double portion of thy spirit be upon me. [10] And he said, Thou hast asked a hard thing: nevertheless, if thou see me when I am taken from thee, it shall be so unto thee; but if not, it shall not be so. [11] And it came to pass, as they still went on, and talked, that, behold, there appeared a chariot of fire, and horses of fire, and parted them both asunder; and Elijah went up by a whirlwind into heaven. [12] And Elisha saw it, and he cried, My father, my father, the chariot of Israel, and the horsemen thereof. And he saw him no more: and he took hold of his own clothes and rent them in two pieces. [13] He took up also the mantle of Elijah that fell from him, and went back, and stood by the bank of Jordan;" 2 Kings 2:9-13 (KJV)

Who is coming up after you? Who will take over your business if something happens to you? Those are some serious questions that as a business owner you have to ask yourself. For the first eight years of my business, I focused on building my business. I was making sure that my clients were happy, I was profitable, learning much and moving forward with the business of next. One day a client asked me about my travels and if I should die while travelling, what would happen to them as the client, and the overall business. I realize that it was a selfish question on the part of the client, but it was a serious question as well. If I were alone and died, my husband would handle my business because I have no biological children: but because my husband and I both have retired from our daily jobs, we travel together. So, I had to look at that critically and determine the who, what, and how of my business if something did happen to me. Most importantly, the who? I have two successors: one who is my comrade in business, and another who is younger, whom I have trained, mentored, and coached. I wanted my clients to have two options just in case either of my options decided that they didn't want to publish any more. Either of these options for my succession are not me. I don't expect them to be me. I want them to be themselves but hopefully, understanding me and what I offer my clients will help them in their decision making and services that they offer to my clients if I'm not here. Hopefully, I have had a positive influence on them and how they treat their own clients that I will never meet. Succession is necessary in all businesses, so consider mapping out, and writing down your business succession plan. Our society, industry, and businesses will be stronger, because we have passed down to the next generation the mistakes, pitfalls, and hardships that we faced and overcame so that they don't have to. Don't wait, start today. Who's next?

Affirmation: God guide, instruct, and notify me of the person that is to succeed me. Help my eyes to be open, my heart to be receptive, my ego to remain in check, and my hand to let go of the reins when it is time. In Jesus' name. Amen.

Question: Who is your successor?

Mentoring and Being Mentored

"Preach the word; be instant in season, out of season; reprove, rebuke, exhort with all long suffering and doctrine." 2 Timothy 4:2 (KJV)

Who is your mentor and who are you mentoring? Being mentored is different than succession. Succession is when someone takes over your spot, in your place, and hopefully, on to the next level and dimension. You can mentor or be mentored by someone else virtually, or in-person, and/or online without ever having met that person. I have several people that I have met over the years that have mentored me and didn't know. Their business skills, ministry, and/or organizational structure have been a model for mine, yet we have never had a conversation. I've bought their books, watched their videos, television shows, webinars, and courses online but have never had a one on one conversation. Would I like the meet them? Sure, I would, but sometimes God will have you model their business behavior without ever having met them in-person. Why? In my case, God said that when I arrive at my destination and/or destiny, it will be because of Him and not because of Mr. or Ms. Whomever. On the other hand, there is nothing like having in-person, one on one mentorship. It is a great feeling when you can text, call, or meet with your mentor face to face, hug them, and break bread with them. Paul, in the above scripture, had a younger pastor and ministry mentee who was named Timothy. Timothy was probably young enough to be Paul's son. He had a goodly heritage in that he was well raised by his mother, and grandmother, but Paul was giving him some final instructions on pastoring and taking care of God's business. Paul knew that it was almost time for his departure, and he wanted to leave his mentee some great instructions for him to follow as he continued in ministry and prepare for the uncertainties that he would surely face. This charge is used in many installation, ordination, and succession services especially for those in ministry. I am not the overseer of a ministry per se, but for me, business has become my ministry. So, I charge each of you to seek God daily as to who to be mentored by, or who you should be mentoring. Take care of your clients, walk in fairness, faithfulness, and forgiveness with each experience that happens in your business. Be willing to negotiate, network, and say no when necessary. When someone asks you to mentor them, ask God but also be willing. Don't compete, and keep your ego in check. We need each other to survive and thrive. Iron still sharpens iron.

Affirmation: Father I thank you that you are my ultimate mentor and I mark you as the perfect man. But you have also given me in-person, human mentors from whom I can learn and glean. Help me to be a mentor to whoever you send my way. In Jesus' name. Amen.

Question: Who is My Mentor? Who am I Mentoring?

Who Is on Your Team?

"Jesus answered them, Have not I chosen you twelve, and one of you is a devil?" John 6:70 (KJV)

If Jesus needed a team, you will need a team. Personally, I am a huge team player but building and sustaining a team is hard for me. Why? Because I usually see greatness in others, impart their ability to succeed in them, and then they leave me to start their own entities which I am fine with, but over time, I realize that to do anything great on a large scale, you have to have a team. Pray for me. I'm working on that in my life. You can't be everywhere, doing everything, because something won't get done, and you'll be sick or dead. So, let's look at Jesus' team.

We don't have the benefit of being both human and divine, only Jesus was, but we can learn from him, the master teacher. He had such a diverse group on His team, some we know a lot about, such as the inner circle: Peter, James, and

John. Others we know little about but they were there with Jesus for the three years of his earthly ministry. Peter was the hot head and always ready to fight, but was still intuitive and filled with discernment when it came to knowing who Jesus really was. John was the humanitarian and gentle soul of the group. There was Matthew who would have been widely known because he was a tax collector, but definitely not well liked. I would love to ask Jesus Himself why He chose Judas. More importantly, Judas was the treasurer, so he must have been good with holding the money because scripture never says that money went unaccounted for; but he still betrayed Jesus, so he wasn't loyal until it was too late. The rest were businessmen, and a support system for Jesus and His ministry. Even if they didn't have a huge role in ministry, they were still there when He fed the five thousand men. This number did not include women and children who were there when He healed the sick and raised the dead. This shows loyalty. Now, He had the team of twelve, but He also had an inner circle of three that were allowed to see things that the other nine did not see, or experience. Some people say that it is 'playing favorites.' I believe and know that everyone can't handle everything and every situation. Jesus taught us that with His team, and we must realize it on our Team.

Know your team members. Know their strengths, and weaknesses, and where they are best suited for certain situations.

Make sure that you explain and share the vision often.

After each experience or encounter, there may have to be times for 'teachable moments' like they taught us in school. It may not be a part of the lesson, but take advantage of teachable moments which can at times, transform a child's life.

Everyone has a part to play in the plan whether it is on the big stage or behind the scenes. Realize that you can't do what you do up front and out front without the great efforts and continuity of your team besides, behind, and out of your sight.

Jesus' team was walking with Him for 3 years, but they did not impact the world until they remembered his teaching, modeled his love, and was empowered with the Holy Spirit. Make sure that your team members have the Holy Spirit, and somehow catch your spirit, so that you can impact the world.

Affirmation: Jesus I thank you for the example of a diverse team. Help me to work with who you send me for the ability to catch and carry out the vision, and not for their outward appearance. In Jesus' name. Amen.

Question: What's most important to me with building a team are three things: trust, skill, and loyalty. What are three most important things for your team members to possess if they are on your team?

_____
_____
_____
_____
_____
_____
_____
_____
_____
_____
_____
_____
_____
_____
_____
_____
_____

Reflection and Planning

_____
_____
_____
_____
_____
_____
_____
_____
_____
_____
_____
_____
_____
_____
_____
_____
_____
_____
_____
_____

Platform, Performance, and Purpose

"Therefore, whosoever heareth these sayings of mine, and doeth them, I will liken him unto a wise man, which built his house upon a rock:" Matthew 7:24 (KJV)

"For the Son of man is come to seek and to save that which was lost." Luke 19:10 (KJV)

"Jesus answered, Thou sayest that I am a king. To this end was I born, and for this cause came I into the world," John 18:37 (KJV)

It's not the logo, brand colors, or the first product that you will launch in your business that's most important. These things are what I call accessories, and not the main things to be concerned about in business. After you have established, and have a consistent relationship with God, the next things are your platform: what are you building, what does God want you to do, and why are you here? It doesn't matter what order you ask Him the questions just be sure and ask Him these three things.

Your Platform should always be built on Him, His Plan, His Ways and finally, Him. Everything else will fail you, bottom line. Whether on purpose, or through outside forces, nothing is forever but God. We stand on Him, His Word, His Promises, His Power, and His Sovereignty. We have our part to play but for us to move as a Christian Entrepreneur we have to build on Him, the Rock and sure Foundation.

Jesus came to seek and to save those that were lost. That was His performance mantra and duty. What is yours? Is your business registered as a for-profit or non-profit? Are you feeding and sheltering the homeless, or just contributing part of your other business profits to help? Are you partnering with someone else who has a homeless ministry? What are you to be doing yourself, instead of copying what someone else is doing? Whatsoever you do shall prosper, but it may not prosper you like it is prospering someone else if it is not for you to be doing in the first place? What should you be doing: ask the

Foundation, the Platform, and the Rock; The Father?

Finally, once you know your purpose, you won't let anything, or anyone stop you. Jesus' ultimate purpose was in His final accomplishment on the Cross - His payment for sin as the Savior of the world. There were many distractions and hinderances, including His inner circle team member, Peter, but Jesus commanded him by saying, "Get thee behind me, Satan." Now, Peter wasn't the devil, but the spirit of the enemy was working through him to try to persuade Jesus to not go to the cross. This was already the most horrific sacrifice and duty for Jesus to do, but it was His Purpose. "For this cause, was I born." You will have people try to persuade you from fulfilling your purpose but you have to ignore them, as much as Jesus did, so that you can fulfill your purpose on the earth.

Build your Platform on a Rock, Ask the Rock what you should be doing, and finally, Ask the Rock, what is your Purpose, and run to it each and every day.

Affirmation: Father I thank you that you are my Platform, my Rock, and my Foundation; you will tell me what, and how to perform; and I know that you have a purpose for me on this earth while I live. Give me the strength to discover, develop, and do it with everything that is within me. In Jesus' name. Amen.

Question: What should you be doing?

Reflection and Planning

How Do You See Yourself?

"And he said unto him, Oh my Lord, wherewith shall I save Israel? behold, my family is poor in Manasseh, and I am the least in my father's house." Judges 6:15 (KJV)

"…we were in our own sight as grasshoppers, and so we were in their sight." Numbers 13:33 (KJV)

"For whosoever exalteth himself shall be abased; and he that humbleth himself shall be exalted."
Luke 14:11 (KJV)

Keeping yourself balanced in this world is very difficult. You should have confidence but not arrogance. You should 'humble yourself under the mighty hand of God' but as a visionary, there will be times that you have to be ready to rise to the occasion when called upon. As a leader, you should command the stage that you are on, but realize your lane, call, time, and place to take the stage, versus when it is time to serve others. It is a balancing act and process.

Every day that you wake up, you see the man or woman in the mirror and must face the fact of who you really are: not what someone else says you are to be; not false humility with an ulterior motive that's masking anger, hidden resentment and revenge; not low self-esteem that lashes out and creates chaos and self-sabotage because you are afraid to succeed. Recognize the person that you were really meant to be, called to be, and established by God Himself to be in this world. "For our righteousness is as filthy rags," we are made righteous and good by God and not by ourselves. Our prayer should be, help me to see myself like you see me, God, and not as the world sees me, or how I see myself.

There are times when God is going to give us an assignment that will be overwhelming to us, and cause us to feel like the Israelites, as a grasshopper, or poor, and the lowest, but if God calls you, it doesn't matter what others think or even what you think of yourself. Walk in what God calls you, and the assignment that He has for you. It will take time. You will make mistakes. You will have to have some long talks with God about it, and then tell yourself to be quiet and listen to God. There will be times when we will have to just trust God and do it despite being afraid, and in spite of the what the man in the mirror feels like, or thinks of himself. We have to override those 'feels' that you see with your natural eye, and see what God sees with your spiritual eye. What does God see in you that you cannot see in yourself? That's the truth of God that lives inside of you and not the lie of your past, other people's ideas, or even your own words that you use to talk yourself out of what God has for you. God give me your eyes so I can truly see what you see.

Affirmation: Father I thank you that you are revealing unto me my assignment and purpose, more each and every day. Help me to trust you, and truly walk by faith and not by what I see. In Jesus' name. Amen.

Question: How does God see you? Ask Him and let Him tell you.

_____
_____
_____
_____
_____
_____
_____
_____
_____
_____
_____
_____
_____
_____
_____

Count up the Cost

"For which of you, intending to build a tower, sitteth not down first, and counteth the cost, whether he have sufficient to finish it?" Luke 14:28 (KJV)

I like to be able to pay for what I order. I like to see the menu even before we arrive at the restaurant. Why? Because I want to know what the cost is before I get there. What is the price range? Are we just ordering a beverage and appetizers; are we able, within our budget, to get a whole meal; or do we need to split it? I literally count up the cost for each project, event and/or endeavor, to make sure that I have the cost of admission. I don't try to predict the return on my investment because I have been wrong many times. That is one of the dichotomies of being a Christian in business as opposed to someone who only does a venture if there is a high return on the investment. I am not saying for you to enter into any project blindly, but you always have to leave room for God. Trust me, I know. I have too many instances where I invested a lot monetarily, and didn't receive an instant return on investment, but received a great opportunity, and doors to even more opportunities that still have yet to be harvested. Sometimes God doesn't allow me to have the funds to participate, because I am not supposed to participate, and I find out why, later. Sometimes God has allowed me to participate in an event, and I realize that it was purely a faith walk, an act of obedience, a "will you do it?" moment in my business. It takes many months, and sometimes even years, before I see an actual return on the investment, or even the reason why I was to do a particular thing, project, or event. It is the trust factor. Now, let me be clear, don't order up something and ask God to pay for it. That's not what I'm saying. I'm saying if you hear from God there may be a great risk involved, but if you heard from God, HE WILL pay, provide, and/or bring the people to make the way. With God, two plus two doesn't always equal four. With God, sometimes you only need those four people at your event because you will do business with three of them and they will cover the entire expense of the event. Ask me how I know! Count up how much it cost! Count how much you got! If there is a gap in the difference and God said do it, He'll make up the difference, and add some to it.

Affirmation: God you've got me, but I have to listen to you with each investment I make. Guide me and help me to listen to you, and not the outside voices that may waste my investment rather than grow it. In Jesus' name. Amen.

Question: How much does it cost?

It Costs – There is an Investment

"…neither will I offer burnt offerings unto the Lord my God of that which doth cost me nothing. So, David bought the threshingfloor and the oxen for fifty shekels of silver." 2 Samuel 24:24 (KJV)

When I was little girl, I was taught that only salvation is free, because Jesus paid the ultimate price for salvation. He paid it all, and all to Him I owe. The Christian lifestyle costs everything, especially my sacrifice of service unto Him and to His people. Even to this day, I have a problem with volunteer services, and/or intern services in my business, because I feel like I should pay something for it. In the case of an intern, they can't accept wages, pay, or stipend because that is not an internship, that's employment. I often give a raving letter to interns because of this practice. On the other hand, there are people that love to get a lot for nothing, or free. They will attempt to pick my brain for free, then turn around and take that same information and make thousands from it. I have to protect, guard, and defend my investment against robbers of knowledge, skill, and sacrifice that took me years to build, but they want it in a manner of minutes. It cost me something to do what I do. It cost me a lot of man hours, sacrifice, no sleep, no vacations, working weekends, taking online courses, watching webinars, audios, and videos to learn what I know. I have to remind myself, as much as I want to help people, and I do often, there is a limit. As time goes on, the more experience you get, the more projects you participate in, and the more clients you satisfy, will reflect the price that you're able to command. On the other hand, God may ask you to sacrifice the price, the project, and the product for Him at no monetary charge, just sweat equity, mentorship, and/or empowerment. He's done it for me, and I let you know to be on the lookout for Him to do it to you. This is your reasonable service, your sacrifice unto God; showing Him that you can be trusted, and not just with the tithe. Also, that you don't worship your business, your clients, or anything else in front of Him. Jesus paid the ultimate price for you. You owe the ultimate sacrifice right back to Him.

Affirmation: Thank you Lord for allowing me to know, and revere that you paid the ultimate sacrifice for my salvation. Help me to not cheapen my sacrifice to you by not being willing to pay the price that is due. In Jesus' name. Amen.

Question: What was your last, and biggest investment?

Faith in a Storm

> "And he saith unto them, Why are ye fearful, O ye of little faith? Then he arose, and rebuked the winds and the sea; and there was a great calm."
> Matthew 8:26 (KJV)

I didn't like them in school, but the only way you know what you know is by the test. The weekly assignments tell a little if you did the homework, but you could have someone else do it, or you could've worked in a group. It's okay when you are learning and in the budding stages, but we only know what you know, in a storm. You need faith for a storm. When you are faced with a business storm it looks like you are going to drown, all clients will leave, you'll never sell another thing and never recover. That's what fear says, but faith says no matter how it looks, God is with me so all things will work together for my good. My faith has to speak much louder than my fear. Is the storm real? Of course, it is real. Could you drown, lose everything, and go bankrupt? Of course, all of these things and even worse could happen. What could be worse you ask? Winning! Victory is just as scary as losing it all. Remember when you started you had plenty of people telling you that it won't work. Like me, you probably have people do the 'concerned check in' to see how you are really doing, but the way they ask is, "Is she drowning yet?" When I say that I am fine, they usually say, "Are you for real?" They secretly don't want me to be fine, but I am. Why? My faith says I'm fine. My faith says God is with me. My faith, to keep moving and walking until I meet my next client, speaks and yells loudly at me. We are not Jesus, but we have to follow His example and say, "In Jesus' name, not mine, but in Jesus' name, Peace Be Still." He controls the winds, and the waves, and the trials, and tribulations of life. Knowing who to call is the real Faith in a Storm.

Affirmation: Father, I am thankful and grateful that you are always with me. You are the

God of the storm. I leave it in your hands. In Jesus' name. Amen.

Question: What storm did you just leave, or are you in right now? Speak to it in Jesus' name.

_____
_____
_____
_____
_____
_____
_____
_____
_____
_____
_____
_____
_____
_____
_____

The Dry Season

"And he said unto me, Son of man, can these bones live? And I answered, O Lord God, thou knowest." Ezekiel 37:3 (KJV)

As a business owner, I have to make you aware that there will be times during your business when you will experience a dry season. It may not be every aspect of your business, but some parts of your business will either dry up, or not produce the results that you expect. It is inevitable. There will be multiple reasons why you have a dry season that could be related to internal, external, or system forces, but it will happen. In that dry season there are several things that should happen.

- Be honest about what happened.
- Be honest about why it happened. Was it beyond your control, or not?

- Take ownership and not just 'blame ship.' Be a real leader and lead your business out of the dry season.
- What did you learn from the time of dryness?
- What can you do now?
- What will you do different moving forward? Will this part of your business continue, yes or no? Did you promote enough, or not at all?
- Reexamine, Regroup, Reorganize and Re-Launch
- Never Give Up.

Affirmation: Thank you, Lord, that you are with me even in a dry season. Give me a plan, direction, and clarity on what to do next. Help me to have the faith that the dry bones that lie waste in this business can live by your power, and in us. In Jesus' name. Amen.

Question: Have you ever been in a dry season? How did you handle it?

Reflection and Planning

_____

_____

_____

_____

_____

_____

_____

_____

_____

_____

_____

_____

_____

_____

What Do You See?

"And Elisha prayed, and said, Lord, I pray thee, open his eyes, that he may see. And the Lord opened the eyes of the young man; and he saw: and, behold, the mountain was full of horses and chariots of fire round about Elisha." 2 Kings 6:17 (KJV)

As a person who has worn glasses and been severely near sighted for most of my life, my eyesight is most precious to me. When I was younger, buying glasses for my prescription was a major expense for my parents. I didn't fully realize it until I had to buy my own glasses with my own money. But as a business owner, as much as I value my natural sight, I value my spiritual and intuitive sight and insight more than my natural sight. Why? Because without a vision, the people perish. Without a vision, your business will perish. Being able to see what you want your business not to be, is just as important as what you want your business to become. As a business owner, your business plan, vision statement, or mission statement, is not a one-time event. It will happen annually, bi-annually, monthly, and even weekly. Things change so rapidly that your business will have to respond to, and hopefully be proactive to, as well as have foresight to handle those things that are specifically prompted by the Holy Ghost. Do it! Worry about the why, later.

You can read the full story of Elisha and his young protégé, Elijah, and why Elisha asked God to "Open his eyes," but to me that is a daily prayer. Open my eyes so I can clearly see. Give me clarity of speech, tongue, and eyesight to move forward in obedience in spite of what it looks like. I walk by faith and not by sight, but what my natural eye can't see, my spiritual, faith-filled eye sees very clearly. Open my eyes!

Affirmation: Give me the sight to see what you want for me, my business, and my life. In Jesus' name. Amen.

Question: What do you see?

Reflection and Planning

_____

_____

_____

_____

_____

_____

_____

_____

_____

_____

_____

_____

_____

_____

_____

_____

Launch

"Now when he had left speaking, he said unto Simon, Launch out into the deep, and let down your nets for a draught." Luke 5:4 (KJV)

I have many clients that grapple with this concept of launching: launching their book, launching their coaching program, launching their website, launching out to accept an online interview, are hard for some people. So, I understand the hesitance and reluctance to launch. Fear, mistakes, and the possibility of failure, are all part of keeping you from launching. But as a reader of this book, with God in Your Business, know that if He told Peter to launch, He will tell you to launch. Now in Peter's case, as referenced in this scripture, he was accustomed to launching, but Jesus challenged him to launch out into the deep.

So, if you have already launched your business, congratulations, but realize that God will always be challenging you in your faith.

Walk with Him and in your business to launch out in deeper, and uncharted territory. It's how we go from faith to faith, and glory to glory. You can't get there standing on the shore, or hiding the plans in a drawer, or not doing the plan at all. You've got to launch.

Now when launching something new, there will, at times, be unmet and/or low expectations. That's what happened to Peter. They were expert fishermen who knew how to fish but had caught nothing, even though they had been out there all night. So, they were not lazy by any means, because they stayed out there and worked at something while gaining little results, all night! But at daybreak Jesus was on the shore knowing that they had caught nothing. The project didn't give you the results that you expected. Sometimes the class you launch, no one attends. Sometimes the product you launch, no one buys, and it is very frustrating, but realize that at least you launched. Yes, but with no results you want to put away your nets; or in today's terms, never put that graphic or put that landing page link on there again. However, you can't do that, you've got to launch out there again. Launch into uncharted territory. Launch in that group on the day that they give you permission to share your products in their group, and not just for one week, but for several weeks. Somebody needs what you have, but you've got to remember to keep putting it out there, and launch!

Affirmation: Thank you, Lord, that as you told Peter to launch out into the deep, help me to listen to you, and in that deep uncharted territory, launch! In Jesus' name. Amen.

Question: What have you launched lately? What has God told you to launch that you still need to launch?

_____

_____

_____

_____

_____

_____

_____

_____

_____

_____

_____

_____

_____

Other Resources By This Author

- ❖ Building the Dream Team
- ❖ eBooks for Business
- ❖ Everyday Miracles Resource Collection – Book, Workbook and Instructor's Guide
- ❖ From Author to Entrepreneur
- ❖ Message to the Masses
- ❖ Plan B
- ❖ Production Creation – Book and Planner
- ❖ Promote That Book Now
- ❖ Publish That Book Now
- ❖ Write That Book Now

All of these resources and more are available at http://roystonroyalbookstore.com

About the Author

Julia Royston spends her days doing what she loves, writing, publishing, speaking and coaching others to tell, introduce and create ways to deliver their stories and messages to the world. That is her "Why." BK Royston Publishing LLC, Julia Royston.net, Royal Media and Publishing and Royston Book Fairs are the conduits that she and her husband, Brian Royston use to spread the love of reading, writing, books as well as build businesses around the world. To date, Julia has written 55 books, recorded 3 music CDs and Coached 150+ to write and publish books as well as established their own businesses.

She is the Host of the "Live Your Best Life" Podcast.

For the replays visit the BK Royston YouTube Channel at http://bit.ly/roystononyoutube and at http://www.juliaroyston.net/liveyourbestlife sponsored by BK Royston Publishing.

For more information, follow her on social media

Facebook @juliaaroyston

Instagram @juliaaroyston

Twitter @juliaakroyston

LinkedIN @juliaaroyston

TikTok @juliaroyston

or visit www.bkroystonpublishing.com or www.juliaroyston.net for updates and upcoming events.

www.ingramcontent.com/pod-product-compliance
Lightning Source LLC
Chambersburg PA
CBHW031633160426
43196CB00006B/392